Foundations In Accountancy
Recording Financial Transactions (FA1)

TP03-1-05924-0022

First edition 2011, Twelfth edition March 2023

ISBN 9781 0355 0575 3

e ISBN 9781 0355 0665 1

British Library Cataloguing-in-Publication Data

A catalogue record for this book is available from the
British Library

Published by

BPP Learning Media Ltd,
BPP House, Aldine Place,
142-144 Uxbridge Road,
London W12 8AA

www.learningmedia.bpp.com

Printed in the United Kingdom

The contents of this book are intended as a guide and not
professional advice. Although every effort has been made to
ensure that the contents of this book are correct at the time
of going to press, BPP Learning Media makes no warranty
that the information in this book is accurate or complete
and accepts no liability for any loss or damage suffered by
any person acting or refraining from acting as a result of the
material in this book.

Welcome to BPP Learning Media's **Foundations In Accountancy Recording Financial Transactions (FA1) Passcards**.

- They **focus on your exam** and **save you time**.
- They incorporate **diagrams** to kick start your memory.
- They follow the overall **structure** of the BPP Interactive Texts, but BPP's Foundations in Accountancy **Passcards** are not just a condensed book. Each card has been separately designed for clear presentation. Topics are self contained and can be grasped visually.
- Foundations in Accountancy **Passcards** are **just the right size** for pockets, briefcases and bags.

Run through the **Passcards** as often as you can during your final revision period. The day before the exam, try to go through the **Passcards** again! You will then be well on your way to passing your exams.

Good luck!

For reference to the Bibliography of the Recording Financial Transactions (FA1) Passcards please go to: learningmedia.bpp.com and visit the "Student" section.

Contents

1: Business transactions and documentation

Topic List

This chapter defines what a business is and introduces business transactions and some important terminology.

What is a business?

Business transactions

Discounts

Sales tax

Storage of information

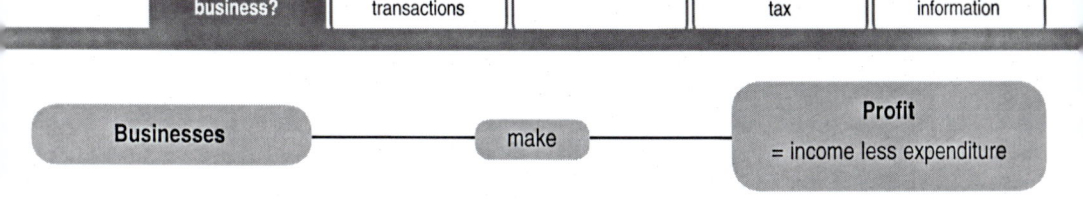

- A business is a **separate entity** from its owner.
- Every financial transaction has a **dual effect**.
- **Double entry bookkeeping** accounts for the dual aspect of financial transactions.

Wherever property changes hands there has been a **business transaction**.

- A **cash transaction** is where the buyer pays cash to seller when goods are transferred.
- A **credit transaction** is a sale or purchase which occurs **earlier** than cash is received or paid.

Business transactions are recorded on documents. These are the source of information in accounts and include:

- Letter of enquiry
- Quotation
- Sales/purchase order
- Delivery note
- Inventory list
- Supplier list

- Staff timesheet
- Goods received note
- Invoice
- Credit note
- Till receipt
- Cheque

> Invoices and credit notes are important documents which must contain **specific** information.
>
> - An **invoice** is a demand for payment.
> - A **credit note** is used by a seller to cancel part or all of previously issued invoice(s).
>
> If it helps, think of a credit note as a negative invoice.

The **accounting system** records, summarises and presents the information contained in the documentation generated by the transactions.

A **discount** is a reduction in the price of goods below the amount at which those goods would normally be sold to other customers of the supplier.

Trade discount	**Settlement (cash) discount**
▪ A reduction in the amount of money demanded from a customer	▪ An optional reduction in the amount of money payable by a customer
▪ Usually results from buying goods in bulk	▪ Given for immediate or very prompt payment
▪ Given on supplier's invoice	▪ Financing decision
▪ No separate accounting required	▪ Needs to be recorded separately in the accounting records

Sales tax

Administered by tax authorities Is an indirect tax levied on the sale of goods and services → Can have a number of rates, eg standard rate, reduced rate

Output sales tax

Sales tax charged by the business on goods/services

Greater than input?
Pay difference to tax authorities

Greater than output?
Refund due to business

Input sales tax

Sales tax on purchases made by the business

Storage of information

Paperwork must be properly handled to ensure **security** and **availability** of information.

A **retention policy** sets down for how long different kinds of information are retained.

Files of data may be **temporary, permanent, active** and **non-active**.

Information no longer needed on a daily basis is **electronically scanned** for long-term storage, **archived** or **securely destroyed**.

Information stored about individuals is regulated by **Data Protection legislation**.

2: Assets, liabilities and the accounting equation

Topic List

The accounting equation

Trade receivables and payables

Double entry

Asset expenditure and expenses charged to profit or loss

This chapter introduces the fundamentals of accounting. It is essential you understand these topics as they form the basis of your studies of financial accounting. You will always be asked to demonstrate your knowledge of double entry bookkeeping. You also need to distinguish between asset expenditure and expenses charged to profit or loss.

The **accounting equation** says:

$$\text{Assets} = \text{Capital} \quad \text{plus} \quad \text{Liabilities}$$

- **Asset** – something which a business **owns** or has the use of
- **Liability** – something which the business **owes** to someone else
- **Capital** – investment of funds to earn a return. Capital is **owed to the owner**
- **Drawings** – amounts of money taken out of a business by its owner

Trade receivables and payables

Trade receivables

A customer who buys goods on credit and pays for them at a later date

This is an asset.

Trade payables

A person to whom a business owes money

This is a liability.

2: Assets, liabilities and the accounting equation

Basic principles

Double entry bookkeeping is based on the same idea as the accounting equation.

- Every accounting transaction has two equal but opposite effects.
- Equality of assets and liabilities is preserved.

Therefore, in a system of double entry bookkeeping, every accounting event must be entered in ledger accounts both as a debit and as an equal but opposite credit.

Debit

An increase in an expense
An increase in an asset
A decrease in a liability (or capital)

Credit

An increase in income
An increase in a liability (or capital)
A decrease in an asset

Asset expenditure

To improve or acquire non-current assets
Creates or increases non-current assets

VS

Expenses charged to profit or loss

For maintenance or trade of the business
Included within expenses

2: Assets, liabilities and the accounting equation

Notes

3: Recording, summarising and posting transactions

Topic List

General ledger

Double entry

Receivables and payables ledgers

Accounting processes

In this chapter you get to grips with the nuts and bolts of double entry. Once you understand this you will be able to deal with transactions posting in your assessment.

General ledger

Ledger accounting is the process by which a business keeps a record of its transactions:

- In chronological order
- Built up in cumulative totals

The general ledger is an accounting record which summarises the financial affairs of a business. Accounts within the general ledger include the following.

- Plant and machinery (non-current asset)
- Inventories (current asset)
- Sales revenue (income)
- Rent (expense)
- Total payables (current liability)

A ledger account or 'T' account looks like this.

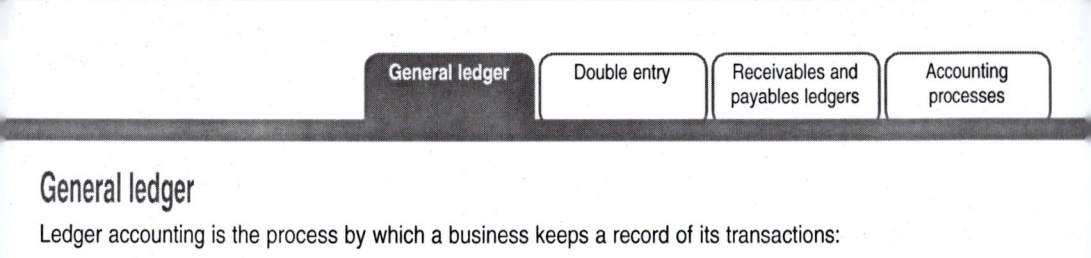

NAME OF ACCOUNT

$	$
DEBIT SIDE	CREDIT SIDE

Double entry

Remember from Chapter 2:

- Every accounting transaction has two equal but opposite effects.
- Equality of assets and liabilities is preserved.

Debit

Increase in expense
Increase in asset
Decrease in liability/capital

Credit

Increase in income
Increase in liability/capital
Decrease in asset

Sales

There are two types of sales transactions:

- Cash transactions where the transaction is paid for at the same time the transaction is made
- Credit transactions where payment is made after the transaction date

All cash transactions go in and out of the bank general ledger account.

Here are the main cash transactions.

Cash transactions	DR	CR
Sell goods for cash	Bank account	Revenue
Buy goods for cash	Purchases	Bank account
Pay an expense	Expense account	Bank account

Cash sale:

BANK ACCOUNT

	$		$
1.1.X1 Revenue a/c	100		

REVENUE ACCOUNT

	$		$
		1.1.X1 Cash a/c	100

3: Recording, summarising and posting transactions

Cash purchase:

BANK ACCOUNT

	$		$
		1.1.X1 Purchases a/c	200

PURCHASES ACCOUNT

	$		$
1.1.X1 Cash a/c	200		

Credit sale:

A credit sale just adds an extra stage.

(i) Sale made on credit

TRADE RECEIVABLES

	$		$
1.1.X1 Revenue	300		

REVENUE ACCOUNT

	$		$
		1.1.X1 Trade receivables	300

(ii) Customer pays amount due

TRADE RECEIVABLES

	$		$
1.1.X1 Revenue	300	31.1.X1 Cash	300

BANK ACCOUNT

	$		$
31.1.X1 Receivables	300		

The trade receivables account now has a zero balance.

Receivables and payables ledgers

To keep track of individual customer and supplier balances it is common to maintain individual ledgers called the receivables ledger and the payables ledger.

Each account in these ledgers represents the balance owed by or to an individual customer or supplier.

Entries to the receivables ledger are made as follows.

In a computerised accounting system, the receivables ledger and the payables ledger are updated automatically when an entry is made against trade receivables or trade payables in the nominal ledger.

The payables ledger operates in much the same way.

Accounting for sales tax

- Records of sales and purchases should **not** include sales tax. Income and expenses are recorded net of sales tax.

- Trade receivables and payables are recorded inclusive of sales tax.

- The sales tax on purchases and sales is recorded in a sales tax account.

- The tax paid to or recovered from the authorities each quarter is the **balance on the sales tax account.**

Computerised accounting

- The principles of a computerised system are **exactly the same as for manual accounting** but the records or files are held in electronic formats.

- Computer activity is divided into **input, processing** and **output**.

- **Batch** processing is where similar transactions are gathered into batches, then each batch is sorted and processed by computer.

- **Control totals** are used to make sure there have been no errors when the batch is input.

- **Computer programs** are the instructions that tell the electronics how to process data. The general term for these is **software**.

- Each account has a unique **code** for identification and posting.

- An accounting package consists of a number of **modules** which perform all the tasks needed and are usually **integrated** with each other.

Data input into one module is automatically transmitted to another relevant module.

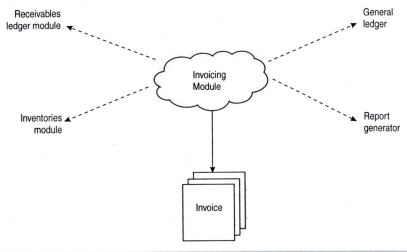

3: Recording, summarising and posting transactions

You should learn the advantages and disadvantages of a computerised accounting system thoroughly.

Advantages	**Disadvantages**
☑ Ability to deal with a large volume of transactions and process them quickly	☒ Danger of unauthorised access to files, security checks need to be set up
☑ Rapid analysis of data to provide useful output which may take a variety of forms, eg invoices, trial balance, aged receivables reports	☒ Danger of data/program corruption
☑ Integration of systems, or modules, prevents wasteful repetition as one entry may update several records	☒ Chance of incorrect/omitted input – system of checks required
☑ Improved accuracy	☒ 'Invisibility' of data
☑ Operators can be non-specialists, as use of codes for input means correct accounts will be updated	☒ Time and cost of installation, training and developing a coding system

4: Completing ledger accounts and financial statements

Topic List

Balancing ledger accounts

The trial balance

The journal

Errors

Financial statements

This chapter looks at the next stage in ledger accounting and the trial balance. It also looks at how errors are dealt with and introduces the principal financial statements that businesses produce.

At the end of an accounting period ledger accounts are totalled up and balanced by the accounting system. However, it is important to understand how this works.

- If the total debits exceed the total credits there is a debit balance on the account.
- If the total credits exceed the total debits then the account has a credit balance.

Balancing ledger accounts

Step 1   Calculate a total for each side of the account.

Step 2   Deduct the lower total from the higher total.

Step 3   Insert the result of step 2 as the balance carried down (c/d) on the side of the account with the lower total.

Step 4   Check that the totals on both sides of the account are now the same.

Step 5   Insert the amount of the balance c/d as the balance brought down (b/d) on the opposite side of the account. This balance b/d is the balance on the account.

Example

This ledger account has a **debit** balance

RECEIVABLES			
	$		$
Sales	10,000	Cash	8,000
		Balance c/d	2,000
	10,000		10,000
Balance b/d	2,000		

A **trial balance** is a list of ledger balances shown in debit and credit columns.

The following steps are taken to put together the trial balance. Note that in a computerised system this is done automatically.

1 Collect together the ledger accounts.

2 Balance the ledger accounts

3 Collect the balances on the ledger accounts in DR and CR columns

Initial trial balance

The balances are then collected in a trial balance.

In a computerised systems debits = credits so the trial balance will always balance.

An example of a trial balance is shown below.

ABC TRADERS		
TRIAL BALANCE AS AT 30 JUNE 20X7	DR	CR
	$	$
Revenue		35,000
Purchases	13,000	
Trade receivables	2,000	
Trade payables		1,500
Cash	10,000	
Capital		10,000
Loan		10,000
Rent	4,000	
Sundry expenses	3,500	
Loan interest	1,000	
Drawings	5,000	
Fixtures and fittings	18,000	
	56,500	56,500

As shown above the trial balance balances. If an accounts assistant was not sure where to record part of an entry they might post it to the suspense account. Any suspense account is **temporary** and must be cleared before the final accounts are produced.

The journal

Journals are used to record any double entries which do not arise from the source documents.

Examples

Period end adjustments

Correction of errors

Large/unusual transactions

Format of journal entries

Date		Debit $	Credit $
DEBIT	A/c to be debited	X	
CREDIT	A/c to be credited		X

Narrative to explain transaction

4: Completing ledger accounts and financial statements

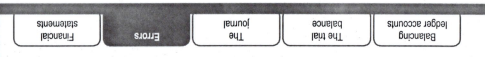

Types of errors

Omission	The transaction has not been recorded at all
Transposition	Two digits in an amount are recorded the wrong way round (eg 245 recorded as 254)
Principle	Recording the double entry in the wrong class of account (eg asset expenditure as expenses charged to profit or loss)
Commission	Accounts assistant makes a mistake when recording transactions (eg posting telephone expenses to the electricity expenses account)
Compensating	Separate errors which are by coincidence equal and opposite to one another

Balancing ledger accounts | The trial balance | The journal | Errors | Financial statements

Businesses produce financial statements to demonstrate how well they have performed over the accounting period (statement of profit or loss) and to show their financial position at the end of that period (statement of financial position).

ABC LTD
STATEMENT OF PROFIT OR LOSS FOR THE YEAR
ENDED 31.12.20X0

	$	$
Sales revenue		X
Cost of sales		(X)
Gross profit		X
Selling costs	X	
Distribution costs	X	
Administration expenses	X	
		(X)
Profit/loss for the year		X/(X)

ABC LTD
STATEMENT OF FINANCIAL POSITION AS AT
31.12.20X0

	$
Assets	X
Capital	X
Liabilities	X
	X

Assets and liabilities are classified as non-current (long-term) or current (short-term).

Notes

5: Receiving and checking money

Topic List

Receipts

Cash transactions require proper processes and documentation.

Receipts

Receipts have to be well controlled to ensure a good cash flow. There are three key features of control.

- **Banking** (performed promptly and correctly)
- **Security** (avoiding loss or theft)
- **Documentation** (remittance advice)

Trade customers usually send a remittance advice with their payment.

> **Till receipts** or **written receipts** are *prima facie* proof of purchase and they must contain certain information.

There are various ways a company can receive money. The main ones are:

- Cash
- Cheque
- Debit or credit card, or digital payment methods

The timing and types of receipt a business experiences will depend on:

- The type of business
- The type of sale
- Seasonal and economic trends

Holding cash creates problems and careful **security procedures** are required.

Strict procedures should be followed when accepting a personal cheque as payment.

Strict procedures should also be followed when accepting **credit, debit or digital payment methods** as payment.

EFTPOS is a means of allowing a transaction to be **recorded immediately** on customer bank accounts or credit card statements, while at the same time **authorising** the transaction.

Controls over the **recording** of cash receipts include:

- Segregation of duties
- Bank reconciliations

Cash registers can be very useful in the control of cash receipts. They are accurate and they can be used to collect different kinds of sales information.

Cash received sheets, or remittance lists are used to collect receipts ready for recording.

Notes

6: Banking monies received

Topic List

The banking system

Banking receipts

You need to understand the banking system and be able to deal with the practical aspects of banking.

The banking system in the UK consists of:

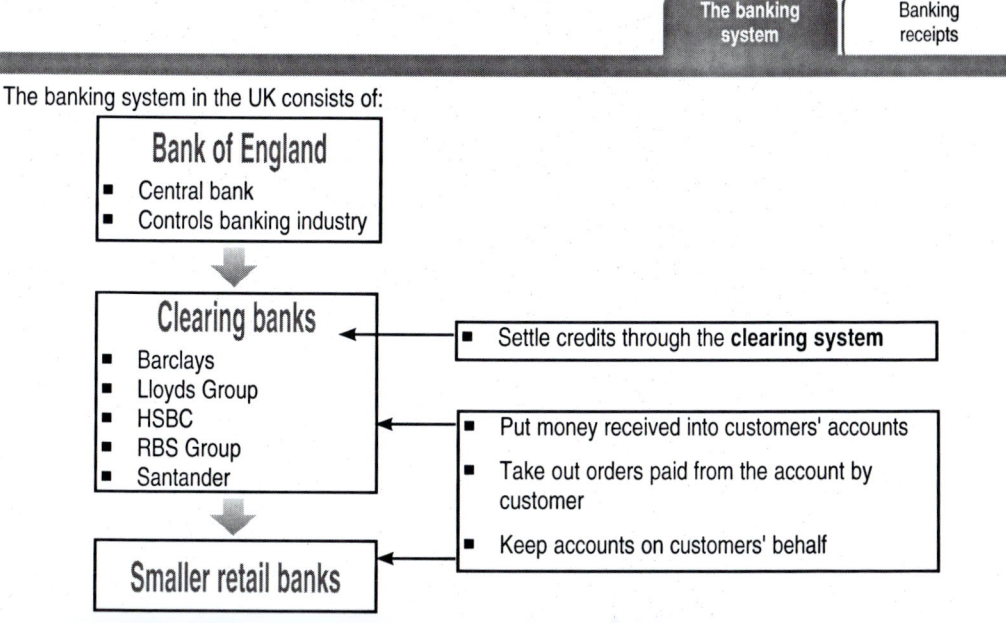

Bank of England
- Central bank
- Controls banking industry

Clearing banks
- Barclays
- Lloyds Group
- HSBC
- RBS Group
- Santander

- Settle credits through the **clearing system**

- Put money received into customers' accounts
- Take out orders paid from the account by customer
- Keep accounts on customers' behalf

Smaller retail banks

Contractual relationship	Transaction	Bank	Customer
Receivable/payable	Customer deposits cash at bank	Receivable	Payable
	Bank gives customer money on overdraft	Payable	Receivable
Bailor/bailee	Customer stores property in bank's safe deposit facilities	Bailee	Bailor
Principal/agent	Bank arranges insurance for customer	Agent	Principal
Mortgagor/mortgagee	Bank lends money to customer with a mortgage on customer's property as security	Mortgagee (Payable)	Mortgagor (Receivable)

Rights of bankers

- Making charges or commissions
- Using customers' money
- Demanding repayment of overdrawn balances
- Possessing a lien over securities

Duties of bankers

- Honour a customer's cheque
- Receipt of customers' funds
- Repayment on demand
- Comply with customers' instructions
- Provide a statement
- Confidentiality
- Advise of forgery
- Care and skill
- Closure of accounts

Duties of customer

- Ensuring fraud is not facilitated when drawing cheques and other funds
- Indemnifying the bank when it acts on the customer's behalf

Banking receipts

Banking cash

Cash must be properly **counted and sorted**

Notes and coins must be listed by denomination on the paying-in slip

Use security procedures

Banking card transactions

Card transactions which are processed manually must be listed on a summary voucher for banking purposes.

The processing copies are sent to the bank while the retailer retains two copies of each voucher (including the summary voucher).

Banking cheques

The details required on the paying-in slip include:

Name of drawer (or endorser)

Amount of cheque

Total value of cheques banked

Number of cheques banked

EFTPOS

Credit, charge or debit card receipts via EFTPOS are credited directly to the retailer's bank account. The retailer can then agree the amounts received to the 'end of day' reconciliation produced by the terminal.

Notes

7: Recording monies received

You will need to be able to record cash received in the accounts of the business. An exam question is very likely to test this.

Recording receipts

The first place a receipt might be recorded:

Cash registers

- Update the computer automatically as sale takes place

- Records total of daily sales which is used to **check** the amount of money in cash register and to **record receipts** in the accounting system

- Security and controls are needed

Cash received sheets

- Used to collect receipts ready for recording

Controls over recording receipts

- Segregation of duties
- Bank reconciliations

Recording cash receipts

Cash sale:

Dr Bank account (gross amount)

Cr Sales (net amount)

Cr Sales tax control account (Sales tax)

Cash received from credit customer:

Dr Bank account

Cr Trade receivables

Note: We don't record any sales tax on receipt of cash from a credit customer as any sales tax would have been recorded when the sale was initially posted to the accounting system.

Notes

8: Authorising and making payments

Topic List

Controls over payments

Payment methods

You should understand the need for proper procedures and documentation when making payments.

Controls over payments

Documentation (invoice, statement, cheque requisition form, expenses claim form)

Authorisation of the expenditure item (passing it for payment)

Authorised signatures for cheques and payment instructions to banks

Cheque requisition forms are used when primary documentation such as an invoice has not been received. Cheque requisition forms help to ensure authorisation and recording of payments.

Expenses paid by an employee for which reimbursement is required are itemised on an expenses claim form.

It is important to establish proper authorisation procedures, with each person in authority having written limits.

A business will use a variety of **methods to make payments**. Ignoring payroll (wages and salaries) and petty cash, the most common and convenient methods of payment are by **debit or credit card** and by **BACS**.

Card payments

Your organisation may have company credit cards.

Other payment methods

Banker's drafts
Standing orders
Telegraphic or interbank transfers
Online transfer

Direct debits

Direct debits authorise an organisation to collect varying amounts from the bank account (but only if the customer has been given advance notice of the amounts and dates of collection).

The **timing of payments** may depend on credit terms offered by suppliers, including discounts for prompt payment.

A business should send proper **explanatory documentation** with all payments to avoid confusion.

The **accounts department** must:

- Make all payments and send these to suppliers with associated documentation (remittance advices and so on)

- Have a system for being able to trace each payment in the event of subsequent queries, for example:

  - Stamping invoices PAID with the date of payment and method of payment

- Keep a filing system for paid and unpaid invoices, standing orders, credit card company statements and any other documentation

- Record payments in the accounts

9: Recording payments

Topic List

Controls over recording payments

Recording payments

You should understand how payments are recorded in the accounting system.

Controls over recording payments are important to **avoid fraud** and to **ensure completeness**.

Controls to avoid fraud
■ Bank reconciliation
■ Authorisation of payments
■ Supporting documentation
■ Segregation of duties
■ Check for unusual payments
■ One cheque book in use

Controls to ensure completeness
■ Regular bank reconciliations
■ Cheques used in sequence
■ Check all payments by direct debit and standing order are recorded

Some organisations still use company cheques, but these are now rare.

Recording cash payments

Cash purchase:

Dr Purchases (net amount)

Dr Sales tax control account (Sales tax)

Cr Bank account (gross amount)

Cash paid to credit supplier:

Dr Trade payables

Cr Bank account

Note: We don't record any sales tax on payment of cash to a credit supplier as any sales tax would have been recorded when the purchase was initially posted to the accounting system.

Notes

10: Maintaining petty cash records

You need to understand how to record and account for petty cash and explain correct procedures.

Petty cash

- Used to make **small payments** with notes and coins
- Cash must be kept **safe** in a **locked box or tin**
- Its security is the responsibility of a **petty cashier**
- Payments must be properly **authorised**

- All transactions must be supported by **receipts** and **vouchers**
- At regular intervals, details of payments are recorded from the vouchers into the **accounting records**

Imprest system

The amount of petty cash is kept at an agreed sum or **float** by topping up from the business bank account.

	$
Cash still held in petty cash	X
Plus voucher payments	X
Must equal the agreed sum or float	X

Topping up the imprest

Step 1	Total the payment and receipt vouchers in the petty cash tin along with any IOU's.
Step 2	Count the cash in the petty cash tin. Check the amount needed to top up equals the total of voucher payments.
Step 3	Prepare a cheque requisition form and have it authorised.
Step 4	Draw the cash from the bank, specifying the denomination of notes and coins.
Step 5	Record the top up amount in the accounting system.
Step 6	Record the vouchers in the accounting systems to record the expenses.

Notes

11: Bank reconciliations

Topic List

Purpose

Proforma

Example

*The balance on a **business's bank statement** should match that in the **bank general ledger account**. When the balances differ they need to be reconciled.*

Bank reconciliation

A comparison of a bank statement with the bank general ledger account

The bank reconciliation is an important financial control.
The bank reconciliation will invariably show a difference.

Differences on bank reconciliation

Errors

- In calculation or recording
- Must be corrected

Bank charges or interest

- Not informed about until receive bank statement
- Must be accounted for in records

Timing differences

- Cheques recorded as received but not yet cleared
- Payments recorded but not yet gone through bank account
- Should be listed and used in the reconciliation

Proforma bank reconciliation

BANK ACCOUNT

	$		$
Balance b/f	X	Dishonoured cheque	X
		Bank charges	X
		Standing orders	X
Error		Direct debits	X
in balance b/f	X	Balance c/f	X
	X		X
Adjusted balance b/f (*)	X		

	$
Balance per bank statement	X
Less outstanding cheques	(X)
Plus outstanding lodgements	X
Plus/less bank errors	X/(X)
Balance per adjusted cash account (*)	X

*These should now agree

Example

The following is the bank general ledger account of Jack.

BANK GENERAL LEDGER ACCOUNT

Debit 20X0	$	Credit 20X0	$
1 March Balance b/f	150	8 March Spratt	30
6 March Cash	75	16 March Tuffet	15
13 March Jill	17	28 March Spider	29
31 March Humpty	39	31 March Balance c/d	207
	281		281

On 31 March 20X0 he received the following bank statement.

20X0		Debit	Credit	Balance
		$	$	$
1 March	Balance (credit)			150
6 March	Cash		75	225
10 March	Spratt	30		195
13 March	Jill		17	212
15 March	Credit transfer – Bill		16	228
18 March	Tuffet	15		213
31 March	Charges	10		203

Bring the bank general ledger account up to date, state the new balance at 31 March 20X0 and prepare a statement to reconcile the difference between the new up to date balance in the bank general ledger account and the balance in the bank statement on 31 March 20X0.

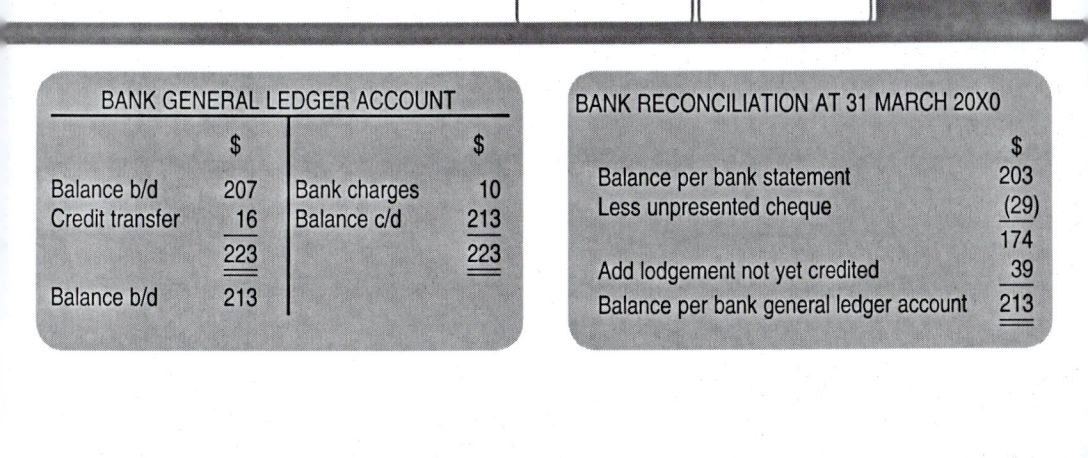

BANK GENERAL LEDGER ACCOUNT			
	$		$
Balance b/d	207	Bank charges	10
Credit transfer	16	Balance c/d	213
	223		223
Balance b/d	213		

BANK RECONCILIATION AT 31 MARCH 20X0

	$
Balance per bank statement	203
Less unpresented cheque	(29)
	174
Add lodgement not yet credited	39
Balance per bank general ledger account	213

12/13: Sales and sales returns and the receivables ledger

Topic List

The accounting system

The receivables ledger

Credit control

You were introduced to sales and receivables ledger in Chapter 3. We now look at these in more detail.

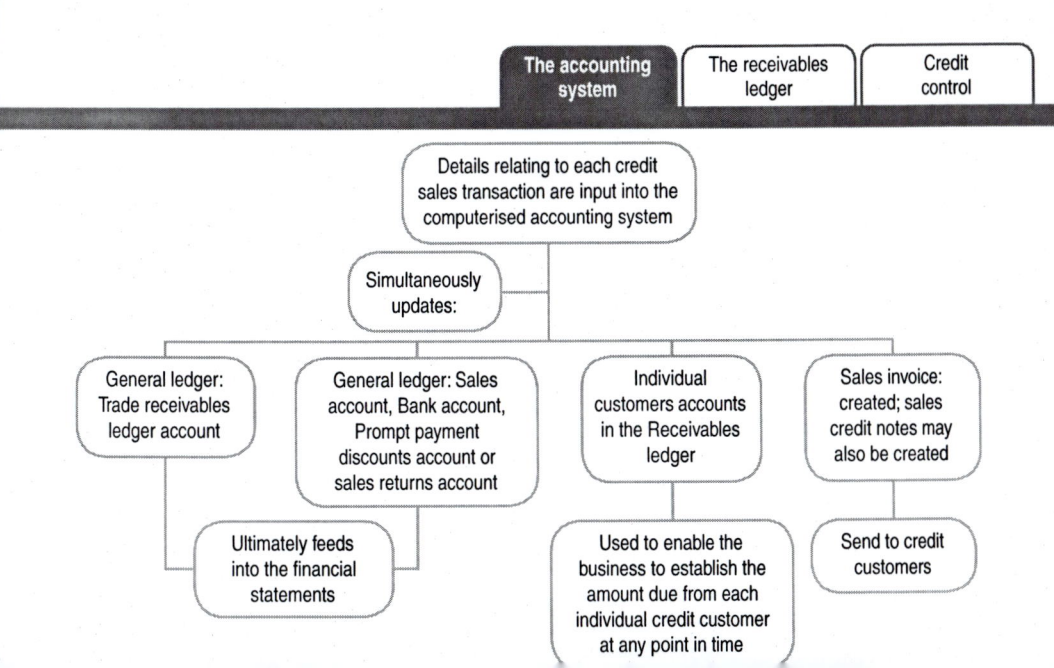

Details relating to each credit sales transaction are input into the computerised accounting system

Simultaneously updates:

General ledger: Trade receivables ledger account

General ledger: Sales account, Bank account, Prompt payment discounts account or sales returns account

Individual customers accounts in the Receivables ledger

Sales invoice: created; sales credit notes may also be created

Ultimately feeds into the financial statements

Used to enable the business to establish the amount due from each individual credit customer at any point in time

Send to credit customers

The **receivables ledger** contains the individual personal accounts for credit customers.

Individual trade receivables accounts

A business needs a record of how much money each customer owes and the items the debt is made up of.

- Statements are sent out each month
- A check can be kept of customers' credit position
- Payments can be matched against debts owed

- There will normally be a debit balance
- They do **not** form part of the double entry system

CUSTOMER ACCOUNT			CU01
	$		$
Invoices sent out inc sales tax	X	Sales returns (credit notes) inc sales tax	X
		Payments received	X

Age analysis of receivables

- Breaks down customer balances on the receivables ledger into different periods of outstanding debt

- Credit controllers can then decide which debts to chase up

- Gives information on the performance of the credit control department

Irrecoverable debts

- There is no real prospect of the debt being paid

- Irrecoverable debts are written off to an irrecoverable debts account in the general ledger

- Authorisation of a senior official is needed

- DEBIT   Irrecoverable debt expense
  CREDIT   Trade receivables

- Individual accounts of the customers whose debts are irrecoverable are taken off the receivables ledger

- Relief can be claimed from sales tax if the irrecoverable debt is at least six months old

14/15: Purchase and purchase returns and the payables ledger

Topic List

The accounting system

The payables ledger

Payments to suppliers

You were introduced to purchases and the trade payables individual ledger in Chapter 3. Now we shall look at these in more detail.

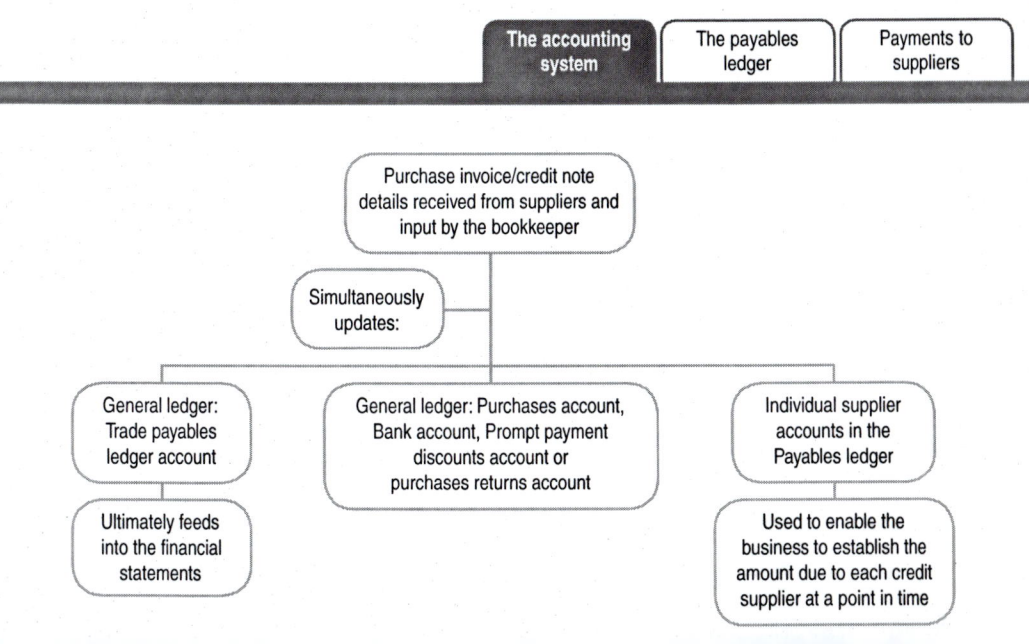

The **payables ledger** contains the individual accounts of suppliers.

Individual accounts

A business needs to maintain an individual account for each supplier.

- To check monthly statements of account from the supplier
- To make appropriate payments on regular basis

- There will normally be a credit balance
- A debit balance may indicate an overpayment or a credit note received after payment made

SUPPLIER ACCOUNT			
	$		$
Payments made	X	Invoices received inc. VAT	X
Purchase returns inc. VAT	X		
Discounts received	X		

14/15: Purchase and purchase returns and the payables ledger

Payments to suppliers

Made on a regular periodic basis

Deciding when and who to pay is a key function of business management

The computerised payables ledger system may print cheques for payment

Checks and authorisation are needed

Age analysis of payables

Shows the age profile of suppliers' balances

It indicates how quickly the business is paying off its debts

The computerised payables ledger will also allow other reports to be printed

Contra entries

Arise if business purchases goods from and sells goods to the same person on credit

There will still be separate accounts in the payables and receivables ledger

Accounts may be settled by **netting off** debts and making contra entries in the accounts

16: Controls over transactions

Topic List

What are general ledger accounts?

Supplier statement reconciliations

Internal checks, sometimes known as internal controls, ensure that transactions to be recorded and processed have been authorised, that they are all included and that they are correctly recorded and accurately processed.

What are general ledger accounts?

Transactions are posted to general ledger accounts in the accounting system. The number of general ledger accounts will depend on the size and complexity of the business. A small business may only have one general ledger account for all their sales, but a larger business may separate sales into a number of different accounts in the general ledger in order to analyse the transactions in more detail. We have already seen general ledger accounts for both trade receivables and trade payables.

Typical entries in a payables general ledger account

		$			$
Cash paid		29,840	Opening credit balances	b/d	8,300
Discounts received		100	Purchases and other expenses		31,100
Returns outwards to suppliers		60			
Closing credit balances	c/d	9,400			
		39,400			39,400
			Credit balances	b/d	9,400

Typical entries in a receivables general ledger account

		$			$
Opening debit balance	b/d	7,120	Cash received		53,700
Sales		52,500	Returns inwards from customers		800
Dishonoured bills or cheques		1,000	Irrecoverable debts		300
			Closing debit balances	c/d	5,820
		60,620			60,620
Debit balances	b/d	5,820			

Supplier statement reconciliations

Suppliers will regularly (monthly or quarterly) send a statement to a customer detailing the transactions in the period and the balance at the end of the period.

The business should reconcile the statements back to the individual trade payables accounts to ensure they are consistent.

Differences should be investigated.

Example supplier statement reconciliation

Mr Smith's individual payables ledger

	$
Original total	16,000
Credit note recorded as an invoice (2 × $500)	(1,000)
Invoice recorded in Mr Stone's account not Mr Smith's in error	2,500
Adjusted total	17,500

Supplier statement from Mr Smith

	$
Original total	19,600
Contra with trade receivables not recorded	(400)
Payment not yet recorded by Mr Smith	(1,200)
Discount not recorded by Mr Smith	(500)
Adjusted total	17,500

17: Recording payroll transactions

Topic List

The nature of payroll

Payroll documents and deductions

Payroll payment

The payroll function in an organisation is very important, as payroll is usually the single highest cost to an organisation.

- A **payroll** is a list of employees and what they are to be paid.

- The wages and salaries bill is of great importance for the employer as it is a major cost.

- Employers have a legal responsibility to collect **income tax**.

The three main requirements for **payroll processing**:

Accuracy
Timeliness
Security

Gross pay is the total pay for the employee's work done in a period.

⬇

Basic pay is the rate for the job.

+

Overtime is payment for work done in excess of standard hours.

+

Commission is often paid to employees who have made a sale. It is normally a percentage of the value of the sale.

+

Bonuses may be paid as a reward for results achieved.

Documents associated with payroll preparation:

- **Timesheets** record the hours spent by each employee on each job.
- **Attendance** records are used by the personnel department to determine reasons for absence from work and to administer the granting of annual leave.
- **Other personnel record documentation** includes cards to record a person's career progress.

Payroll deductions

- Income tax
- Benefit contributions
- Pension scheme payments

A basic computation

	$
Gross pay (what your work has earned you)	1,000
Other (includes statutory sick pay, statutory maternity pay, holiday pay etc)	200
	1,200
Less: Income tax	(140)
Benefit contributions	(100)
Other deductions	(50)
Net pay	910

Payslips

Employees have a legal right to a payslip.

Compulsory disclosures:

- Employer's name
- Employee's name
- Gross pay
- Additions to and deductions from pay
- Employee's pension contributions
- Sick pay

Payment methods

Payments are usually made by cheque or credit transfer.

Many companies now use an automated payment system.

Cash payments have reduced due to:

- Security problems
- Extra time and effort compared to other payment methods

Notes